Separating Solids and Liquids

By the end of this book you will know more about:

- Solids and their properties.
- Liquids and their properties.
- What happens when things melt.
- What happens when things freeze.
- How to separate mixtures of solids and liquids.

You will:

- Plan and carry out a fair test investigation.
- Solve a problem about separating different materials.
- Use books, CD-ROMs and the Internet to carry out research.
- Draw up tables showing the results of experiments.

Identify solids and liquids.

Task 1 *Is it a solid or a liquid?*

✺ What do you know about solids and liquids?
Write down as many different examples of solids and liquids as you can.

✺ Make a list of solids and a list of liquids.

✺ What can you say about all the solids on your list?
How are they the same?

✺ What can you say about all liquids on your list?
How are they the same?

✺ Write down your ideas.

Stone   Water

Oil

Cotton wool   Plastic

Syrup

Flour

Sand   Brown sugar

Extra Challenge

✺ Collect the materials shown in the photograph.

✺ Working in groups, sort the materials out into three sets – **solids** and **liquids** and **not sure**.
How will you decide whether each material is a **solid** or a **liquid**?
If there are any materials about which you can't decide, put them in the **not sure** set.

✺ What did the other groups decide?
Compare your answers.

Powders and granules are made up of tiny solid pieces that you can pour like liquids.

 Task 2 *Looking at powders and granules*

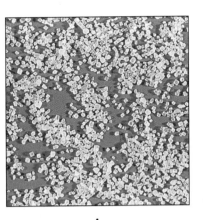

A

B

C

What do you think these photographs show?
Are the materials solids or liquids?

The photos show different materials under a magnifier.

Look through a magnifier at the materials you sorted in Task 1.
Do any of them look like the photographs?

The photographs show salt (A), sand (B) and flour (C).

Powders and granules seem a bit like liquids because you can pour them, but they are really solids.

Powders and granules are made up of tiny solid pieces.

Words to learn and use:
granules
liquid
pour
powders
solid

3

Task 3 — Pouring things

✦ How can you tell a solid from a liquid? Sometimes people say that you can pour liquids, but you can't pour solids.
Test this idea to see if it's correct.

Poured water

YOU NEED:

jug of water

sand

trays or bowls

Poured sand

✦ Pour some dry sand onto a tray or bowl. You have just 'poured' solids. Look at the small mountain shape the sand makes.

✦ Now pour some water into another tray or bowl. Can you make it into a mountain shape?
How is the liquid water different to the solid sand?
Think of each little bit of solid: it stays the same shape and does not flow.
Think of a liquid: it does not stay the same shape but flows easily, spreading out to make a level surface.

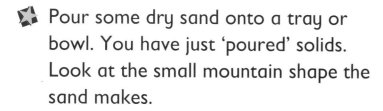

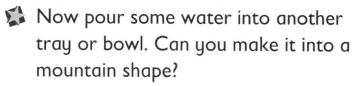

Fact File

Properties of solids

The shape and volume of a solid do not change. If you move a brick or a grain of sand from one container to another, it will still have the same shape and it will take up the same amount of space.

**You can use a measuring cylinder to find the volume of a liquid.
Liquids poured from one container to another may change shape but not volume.**

 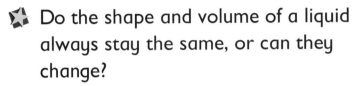 *Shape and volume of liquids*

 Do the shape and volume of a liquid always stay the same, or can they change?

We can find the volume of a liquid with a measuring cylinder.

The surface of a liquid usually goes up a little at the edges where it touches the container.

Where should you measure the volume? At the higher level at the edge of the surface? Or at the slightly lower level in the middle of the surface?

The surface of a liquid in a container

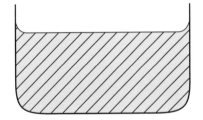

Properties of liquids

The volume of a liquid does not change. If you move a liquid from one container to another, it will take up the same amount of space. But the shape of a liquid does change. A liquid always takes the shape of its container.

YOU NEED:

jug of water

several different measuring cylinders

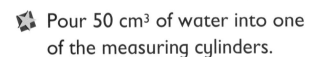 Pour 50 cm³ of water into one of the measuring cylinders.

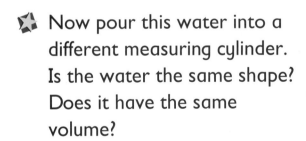 Now pour this water into a different measuring cylinder. Is the water the same shape? Does it have the same volume?

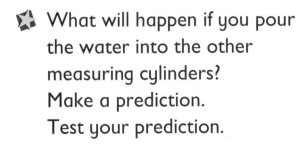 What will happen if you pour the water into the other measuring cylinders? Make a prediction. Test your prediction.

⭐ You can change a solid to a liquid by heating.

Gold

Before heating   *After heating*

Task 5 *Before and after*

⭐ Look at these pictures of gold and cooking fat before and after heating.

Each material changes its appearance when it is heated.

⭐ Describe what each material is like in each picture. Write under these headings:

Cooking fat

Before heating   *After heating*

Gold before heating | Gold after heating

Cooking fat before heating | Cooking fat after heating

Fact File

Melting

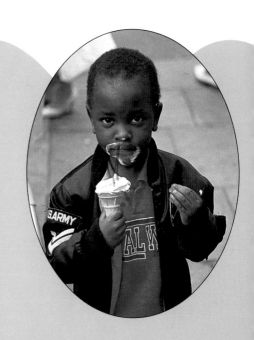

When most solids are heated, they change into liquids. The solid and liquid may look different, but they are still the same material. They have not changed into a new material. When a solid material changes into a liquid form of the same material, we say it melts.

You can change a liquid to a solid by cooling. You can change a solid to a liquid and back to a solid again. This is called a reversible change.

Task 6

Melting wax and melting water
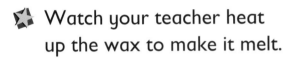

When you heat most solids, they melt and turn into liquids.

✹ Leave an ice cube and a piece of candle wax on a plate.

✹ Watch what happens.

The classroom is hot enough to melt the solid water (ice). It is not hot enough to melt the wax.

✹ Watch your teacher heat up the wax to make it melt.

Solid wax has to be much hotter than solid water before it will melt.

If you want to change liquid water back into a solid, you must put it in a freezer.

You do not have to put liquid wax into a freezer to make it go solid – it will do it in front of you in the classroom.

✹ Watch the wax turn back into a solid as it cools. Wax goes solid, or solidifies, at a higher temperature than water.

You can change wax and water from solid to liquid, and from liquid back to solid again. This sort of change is called a **reversible change**.

Ice Candles

The middle of an ice candle is like a normal candle. It is made of solid wax. The edges of an ice candle are also made of solid wax, but there are holes in the wax.

These pictures show you how an ice candle is made.

1 Prepare the equipment. You need a candle, some ice crushed into large pieces, wax, a mould, a bowl and a saucepan.

2 Put an ordinary candle in the middle of a mould. Put the mould in a bowl. Put crushed ice around the candle.

3 Heat some more wax until it has melted.

4 Pour the hot liquid wax over the cold ice. The liquid wax cools down and turns solid. The ice gets hotter and turns liquid. The water runs into the bowl.

5 Leave the wax candle until it is cool. Take it out of the mould.

⚠ *The wax must be heated and poured by an adult.*

How was the ice candle made?

- Look at the Fact File on page 8.

- Work out the answers to these questions.

- Write your answers on Task Sheet 1.

  - What are the two different materials you need to make an ice candle?

  - Why was the wax heated?

  - What happened to the hot liquid wax when it was poured over the ice?

  - What happened to the ice when the hot liquid wax was poured over it?

  - How were the holes around the edge of the candle made?

  - Which one of the materials used goes solid without going in the freezer?

Cold changes

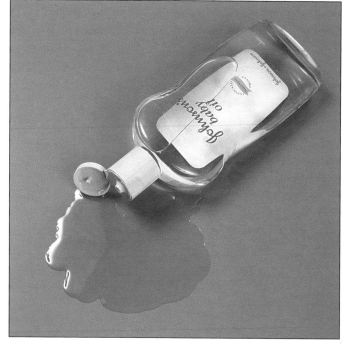

Baby oil

* At room temperature, baby oil is a liquid.
  Could you change baby oil into a solid?

* Suppose you put baby oil into a freezer for a few hours, what do you think would happen?

* Try it.
  What happens?

* Collect some other materials that are liquid at room temperature, such as milk, vinegar and syrup.

* Predict what you think they will be like after a few hours in the freezer.

* Put them in the freezer.

* After a few hours, take them out and describe what they look like.

* Use Task Sheet 2 to write down your descriptions.

* Did all the materials become solid?

* Do all the solids change back into liquids when they are taken out of the freezer?

The temperature machine

✣ Imagine an amazing temperature machine. Turn the dial one way, and everything inside the machine gets colder and colder until it is STUPENDOUSLY cold. Turn the dial the other way, and everything inside the machine gets hotter and hotter until it is STUPENDOUSLY hot.

✣ Now imagine putting some cooking oil in the machine. Turn the dial so that it gets colder and colder. What will happen?

✣ Imagine putting some rock into the machine.
Turn the dial to make it get hotter and hotter. What will happen?

Words to learn and use:
freeze
measuring cylinder
melt
reversible
solidify
volume

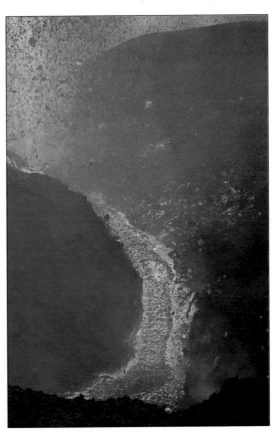

A volcano erupts and lava flows

....

✴ The **melting point** is the name given to the temperature at which a material changes from solid to liquid.
Wax changes from solid to liquid at a higher temperature than ice.
We say that wax has a higher melting point than water.

✴ Use books, CD-ROMs or the Internet to find out the melting points of different materials.

✴ Make a list of the materials and their melting points.

Extra Challenge

✴ Now try to find out the melting points of some of these materials:

Iron

Diamond

Graphite
(the material in the middle of pencils)

Gold

Aluminium

✴ Make a list and put them in order.
Start with the material with the highest melting point.

⭐ **Plan and carry out a fair test investigation, recognise possible hazards and suggest explanations for results.**

Scientific Enquiry

Fast fats

✴ You are going to have a competition between some different types of fat to see how much time they take to melt.

These pictures show you how to do the test.

YOU NEED:

stop-clock   bowl of hot water

foil cases or milk bottle tops

a selection of fats

✴ When you do this test, what will you be changing?

✴ What will you measure?

✴ What will you keep the same to make it a fair test?

✴ What hazards might there be?

✴ How will you make sure that you carry out the test as safely as possible?

✴ Complete the planning board on Task Sheet 3.

✴ Now carry out the test.

✴ Make a table showing how long it takes for each fat to melt.

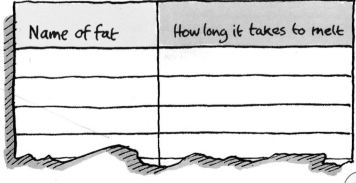

Name of fat	How long it takes to melt

✴ Look at the results on your table.

✴ Which fat was the champion melter and melted in the fastest time?

✴ Which fat came second?
Which fat came third?

✴ The different fats took different times to melt. Why do you think this happened?

✴ Write your answers on Task Sheet 4.

Extra Challenge

✴ Now you are going to put your foil cases of melted fats on top of icy cold water.

✴ Which fat do you think will solidify first? Why have you made your prediction?

✴ Talk about it in your group.

✴ Put the fats on the icy water to test your prediction.

✴ Describe what happens using words and pictures.

✴ Was your prediction correct?

✴ The fats took different times to solidify. Try to explain why this happened.

When solids are mixed, you can sometimes separate them again.

YOU NEED:

packet of
dried soup with
croutons

QUICK SOUP

different sieves

paper towels

Task 12 *Solids in the soup*

- Tip the contents of a packet of dried soup into a bowl.
  You will see that it is made up different solids.

- Using sieves and paper towels, sort the dried soup into piles of different solids.

- Why did some things pass through the sieves while other things didn't?

Extra Challenge

Sometimes we can separate solids without using sieves.

- Mix together some small, torn-up bits of paper and some steel paper-clips.

- Can you think of a way to remove the steel paper-clips from the mixture?

- Try out your idea. Did it work?

- Do you think it would work with plastic paper-clips?
  Explain your answer.

Sometimes when you mix a solid with water, there are changes. If the solid stays mixed with the water, we say it has dissolved.

Task 13

The mixing game

5

- Collect a small amount of each of these solids.

Instant coffee
Sand
Salt
Flour
Chalk powder
Marbles
Plaster of Paris

- Add each solid to a different beaker of water.
- Describe what happens.
- Leave the mixtures to stand. Do they still look the same after an hour?
- Make a table of your results. Show which material you added to water, what happened at first and what happened after one hour. What headings will you use for the columns on your table?

YOU NEED:

several beakers

spoons

water

variety of different solids

Extra Challenge

You have mixed different solids with water.

- Which of these mixtures could you separate?
- Which one has changed into a new material?
- Which solids have dissolved in the water?
- Write your answers on Task Sheet 5.

⭐ **You can separate undissolved solids from a liquid by filtering.**

Going through the holes

⚡ What do you notice about the size of the holes in these sieves?

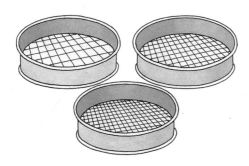

Here are two types of paper.

Kitchen paper

Filter paper

If you looked at each piece of paper under a very strong magnifier, you would see small holes in the paper.

⚡ Do you think the holes in the filter paper and the kitchen paper would be the same size?

You are going to filter some mixtures through both papers.

⚡ To get equipment ready, you must follow these instructions:

YOU NEED:

3 filter papers

3 sheets of kitchen paper

9 beakers

6 funnels

sand

brown sugar

flour

scissors

teaspoon

measuring cylinder

jug of water

1 Collect six funnels, three circles of filter paper, three sheets of kitchen paper and a pair of scissors.

2 Cut a circle from each sheet of kitchen paper. Make it the same size as the filter paper.

3 Fold each paper circle in half and then fold again into quarters.

4 Separate one of the folded edges, to form a cone that fits neatly into a funnel.

5 Place each of your six paper cones in a different funnel.

- Put these three mixtures into different beakers and stir each of them:

  - A teaspoon of sand and 100 cm^3 of water.
  - A teaspoon of flour and 100 cm^3 of water.
  - A teaspoon of brown sugar and 100 cm^3 of water.

- Set up your funnels over six empty beakers.

- Pour some of each mixture through each type of paper.
  What happens?

- Use Task Sheet 6 to record your results.

- Why do you think that some flour goes through the kitchen paper but not through the filter paper?

- If something has dissolved, can you separate it from the water by filtering?
  Explain your answer.

Melting and dissolving

These children are talking about melting and dissolving.

They are trying to work out if melting and dissolving are the same or different.

> You have to get a solid and a liquid mixing for dissolving. There is no mixing needed for melting. They are different.

> I think melting and dissolving are different. You have to make solid things hotter to make them melt. Things will dissolve in cold water.

> ...lt dissolves in ...ds out everywhere. ...nelts, it spreads out ...think melting and ...are the same.

are different because when a solid is mixed with melts it turns to liquid. When a solid dissolves it disappears.

...with them?

Talk about their ideas in your group.

Words to learn and use:
dissolve
filtering
filter paper
flowing
melting point
mixture
separate
sieve

YOU NEED:

beaker

tub of soft margarine

spoon

jug of warm water

Melting or dissolving?

✺ Do you think margarine will melt or dissolve when you pour warm water on it?

✺ Press a blob of soft margarine onto the bottom inside of a beaker.

✺ Slowly add warm water to the beaker.
Watch carefully.
What happens?

✺ Draw three pictures to show what happened to the margarine in the hot water.

✺ Did the margarine melt or dissolve? How could you tell?

✺ What do the words melting and dissolving mean?

✺ Working in pairs, write down your ideas.

✺ What did others in the class say? Compare your answers.

Write instructions for a scientific enquiry. Choose the right equipment and use it correctly. Predict what will happen.

Scientific Enquiry

The big mix-up

You have found out about three ways of separating mixtures.

There has been a big mix-up in the classroom.

In Bowl A, water, sand and marbles are mixed up.

In Bowl B, rice, dried peas and steel paper-clips are mixed up.

Sieving

Filtering

Using a magnet

Bowl A

Bowl B

How could you separate the mixtures?

✹ Plan how you would do it.

✹ Think carefully about each step you will take.

✹ Predict what will happen at each step.

✹ What equipment will you need?

✹ Write two sets of instructions - one for separating the mixture in Bowl A, and one for separating the mixture in Bowl B.

✹ Use Task Sheet 7 and Task Sheet 8 to write down your instructions.

✹ Show your instructions to your teacher.

✹ Now follow your instructions and try to separate the two mixtures.

✹ Did your instructions work?
Were you able to separate the mixtures?

✹ Explain to the class what happened.

Checkpoint

The new pupil

Imagine a new child has just joined your class.

You have to tell him what you have learnt about solids and liquids.

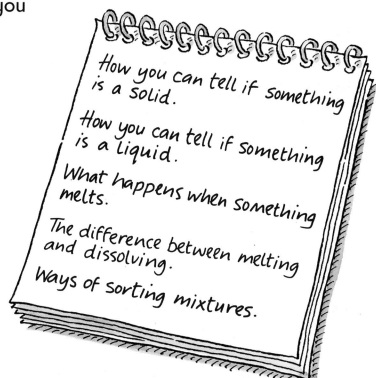

Make notes of the main things you would tell him about.

Remember that notes:

- focus on the main ideas
- use key words
- are short

How you can tell if something is a solid.

How you can tell if something is a liquid.

What happens when something melts.

The difference between melting and dissolving.

Ways of sorting mixtures.

Write your notes under these headings.

Summary

Which of these do you know and which can you do?

- I know how to tell if something is a solid or a liquid.
- I know that powders and granules are made up of tiny solid pieces that can be poured like liquids.
- I know that liquids poured from one container to another may change shape but not volume.
- I can measure volume using a measuring cylinder.
- I can change a solid to a liquid by heating it and change a liquid to a solid by cooling it.
- I know that melting and solidifying are reversible changes.
- I can plan and carry out a fair test investigation, recognise possible hazards, and suggest an explanation for the results.
- I know how to separate different mixtures of materials using filters, sieves and magnets.

Complete your **Science Log** to show how well you know these and how well you can do them. Circle a face for each statement.